Let's Talk About When Your Pet Dies

Marianne Johnston

First published in Great Britain by Heinemann Library,
Halley Court, Jordan Hill, Oxford OX2 8EJ,
a division of Reed Educational & Professional Publishing Ltd.

OXFORD FLORENCE PRAGUE MADRID ATHENS MELBOURNE AUCKLAND
KUALA LUMPUR SINGAPORE TOKYO IBADAN NAIROBI KAMPALA JOHANNESBURG
GABORONE PORTSMOUTH NH (USA) CHICAGO MEXICO CITY SAO PAOLO

Manufactured in the United States of America.

02 01 00 99 98
10 9 8 7 6 5 4 3 2 1
ISBN 0431 03600 4

British Library Cataloguing in Publication Data
Johnston, Marianne
Let's talk about when your pet dies
1. Pets – Death – Juvenile literature 2. Grief in children – Juvenile literature
I. Title II. When your pet dies
155.9'37

Acknowledgements
The Publishers would like to thank the following for permission to reproduce photographs:
Cover photo by Carrie Ann Grippo; page 7 © Dusty Willison/International Stock;
page 12 © Caroline Wood/International Stock; all other photos by Carrie Ann Grippo.
Our thanks to Mandy Ross in the preparation of this edition.
Every effort has been made to contact copyright holders of any material reproduced in this book.
Any omissions will be rectified in subsequent printings if notice is given to the Publisher.

Contents

Words in **bold letters like these** are explained in the Glossary on page 23.

Not just a pet

Susie always looked forward to coming home from school to play with her dog, Chief. Chief had been a part of the family since Susie was a baby. She loved taking Chief for walks and playing catch with him. Chief was Susie's best friend.

Then, one day when Susie came home from school, Chief was gone. Susie's mum said that he had been hit by a car. Susie was very sad. Her best friend had died.

Your pet may have been your best friend.

What is a pet?

A pet is a lot more than an animal who lives in your house. Pets can become part of your family. They can cheer you up when you're unhappy, or keep you company when you're bored. Your pet is an important part of your life.

So losing a pet can be painful and sad. It may feel as if a member of your family has died.

Pets become part of your family. ▶

How pets die

Some pets die in road **accidents**, like Susie's dog, Chief. Others become so ill that they will never get better. They have to be **put to sleep**. This means that the **vet**, or animal doctor, will give your pet an **injection** that helps it to die without any pain.

This may seem like a terrible thing to do. But if your pet is hurting a lot, and it will never get better, it is kinder to put it to sleep than to keep it alive.

Sometimes pets who are ill or hurting have to be put to sleep by the vet.

When you lose a pet

When your pet dies, you lose more than a **playmate**. You lose something that you loved, which was a big part of your life.

You may have many strong feelings when a pet dies. You may be angry and upset. Or you may feel sad and lonely. You may not feel anything at all for a while. It is normal to have any or all of these feelings. Losing a pet is hard.

You may feel sad and upset when your pet dies. It is normal to feel like this. ▶

It's okay to cry

You will probably feel very sad when your pet dies. You may even want to cry. It's okay to cry. Crying is your body's way of getting rid of sadness.

Some people never like to cry in front of others. They are afraid of what other people might think. But crying is the best way to let others know that you are sad – and then they can try to help you to feel better.

Blaming someone

You may be angry when your pet dies. You may want to **blame** someone. If your pet was **put to sleep**, you may blame the **vet**, or your parents. If your pet was knocked down by a car, you may blame the driver of the car.

If you find yourself doing this, remember that blaming people won't bring your pet back. Talk to someone, such as a parent or teacher, about your angry feelings. Talking may help you to feel better.

You may want to take your angry feelings out on your family. But remember that they are sad, too.

Remembering your pet

At first you might try to forget about your pet. Thinking about it can be sad and painful. But you won't start to feel better if you keep your sadness inside.

Talking about your pet will help. It may be hard at first. But soon you will be thinking more about the good times you had together and less about its death. You might even want to put up a photo of your pet in your bedroom.

Trying to forget about your pet will not make the pain or sadness go away.

Funny stories

Once you start to talk about your pet, you will start to feel better. You and your family can share funny stories about your pet, and talk about some of the things you liked best about it.

You can talk about its death, too. Ask your parents about anything you don't understand. You may be **confused** about how or why your pet died. Your parents might have some or all of the answers.

Talking about the good times with your pet can help to make you and your family feel better. ▶

A new pet

You and your family may **decide** to get a new pet. This new pet won't take the place of the one that died. But soon it will have its own place in your heart and in your family.

You may be afraid that this pet will die, too. It is normal to feel this way. But when you think about the good parts of having a pet, you will see that it's worth the **risk** of losing it.

Getting a new pet doesn't mean that you've forgotten the old one. It just means that you have a new pet to love.

Lisa and her cat

Lisa cried for days when her cat died. She missed Tommy so much that she thought the pain would never go away. At first she didn't even want to think about him.

But then Lisa talked with her parents about him. She explained how Tommy used to climb into her bed in the mornings, and nudge his nose against her nose to wake her up. Talking about the good times with Tommy made Lisa feel much better.

Glossary

accident (AK-sih-dent) – something harmful or unlucky that
    happens when you aren't expecting it

blame – to hold someone responsible for something bad or wrong

confused (kon-FYOOZD) – to feel mixed up

decide (dee-SIDE) – to make up your mind

injection (in-JEK-shun) – a jab with a **vet's** or doctor's needle

playmate – friend

put to sleep – when the **vet** helps an animal to die without
    any pain

risk – chance of harm or loss

vet – animal doctor

Index